How to Catch a Lobster

By Leslie S. Moore

© Leslie S. Moore, 2016

Published by

Penobscot Books

a division of Penobscot Bay Press, Inc.
P.O. Box 36, 60 Main St., Stonington ME 04681 USA
penbaypress.me books@pbp.me 207-367-2200

ISBN: 978-0-941238-21-2
LCCN: 2016940245

Printed in the USA by 360 Digital Books, Madison Heights, Michigan

Leslie S. Moore is a pen-and-ink artist and woodblock printmaker in Belfast, Maine, whose first love is drawing pets. Find her website at *PenPets.com*.

To Ed and Anne

First you need
a good lobster **boat**.
Anne Elizabeth will do. She's sleek
and smart and **seaworthy**.

Next you need
a *clever* captain.
Ed Black is a pro.

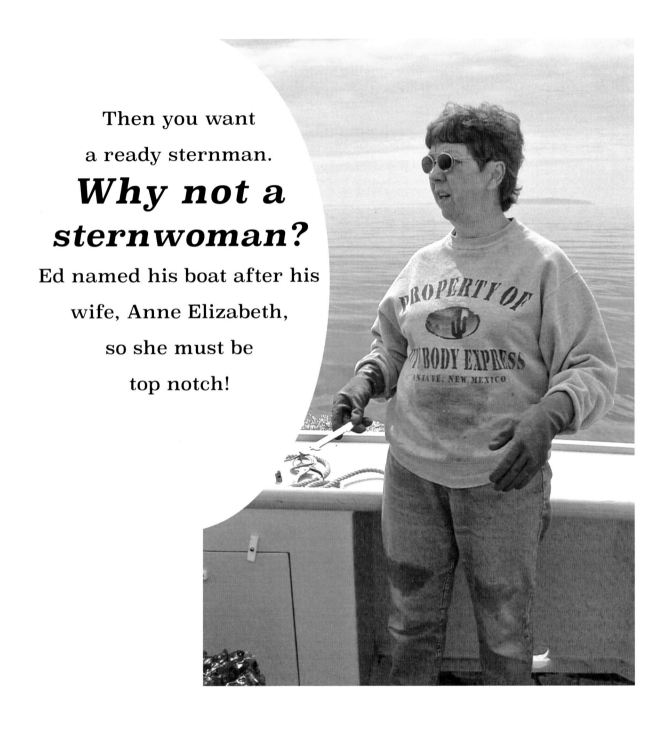

Then you want
a ready sternman.

Why not a sternwoman?

Ed named his boat after his
wife, Anne Elizabeth,
so she must be
top notch!

Finally, how about
a **_salty sea dog?_**
Nickie really knows
the ropes.

Boat and crew **begin the day** at the ***bait shack***, where Ed shovels herring into buckets.

Three buckets **full!** The **fresher** the herring, the better the lobsters like it!

Anne gets right to work stuffing **bait bags** full of fish.

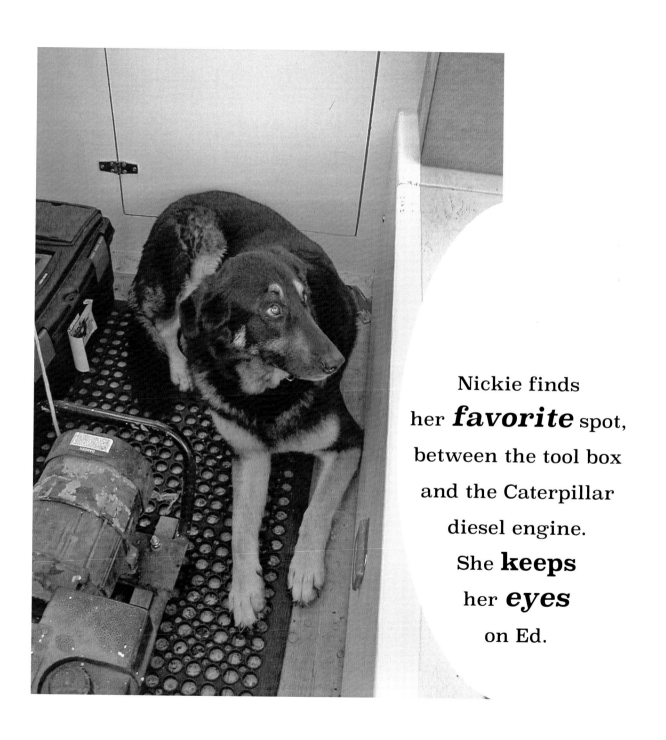

Nickie finds
her ***favorite*** spot,
between the tool box
and the Caterpillar
diesel engine.
She **keeps**
her ***eyes***
on Ed.

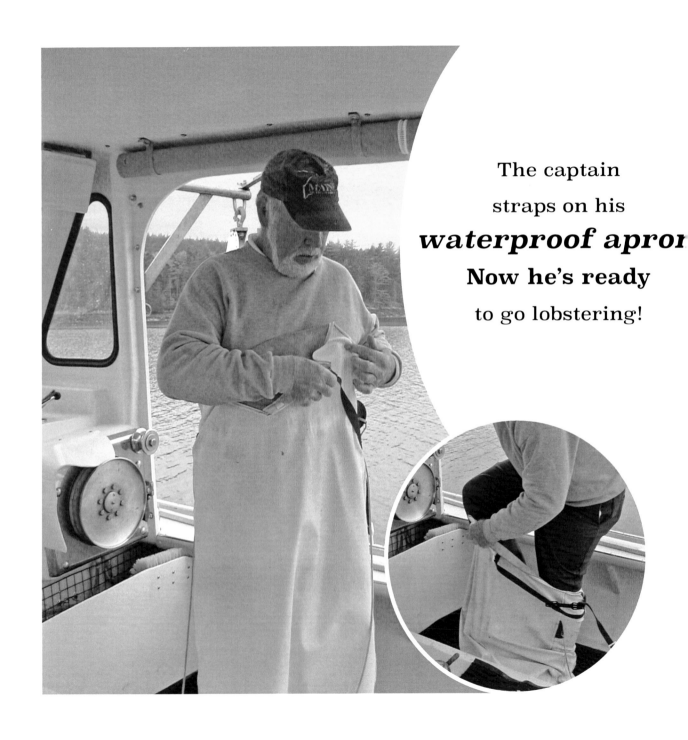

The captain straps on his **_waterproof apron_** **Now he's ready** to go lobstering!

Ed wraps the first *trap line* around his *pot hauler*. **WHIRRRRRRR!**

It hauls

the ***lobster trap***

up from the bottom of the ocean.

And what's inside?

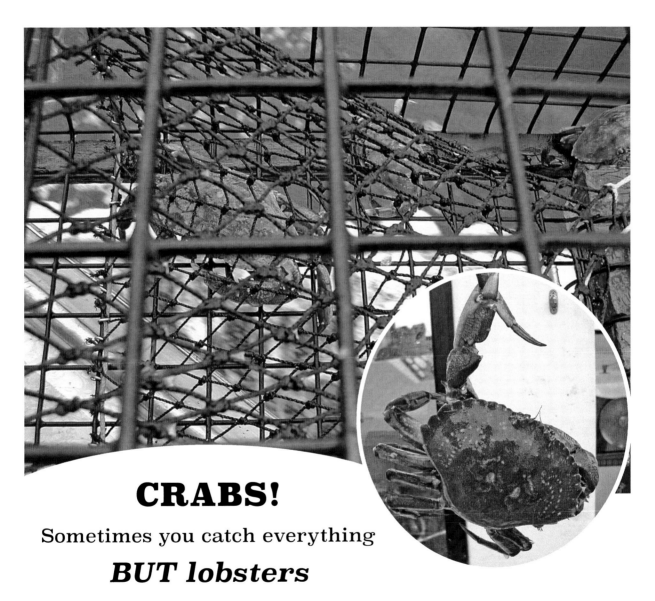

CRABS!

Sometimes you catch everything

BUT lobsters

in your traps.

Sometimes you catch
a **_peekytoe crab_**
who *scowls* at you!

Sometimes you catch
a **rock crab** who
hisses at you!

Sometimes you catch
a ***squiggly eel***.
EEEEK!

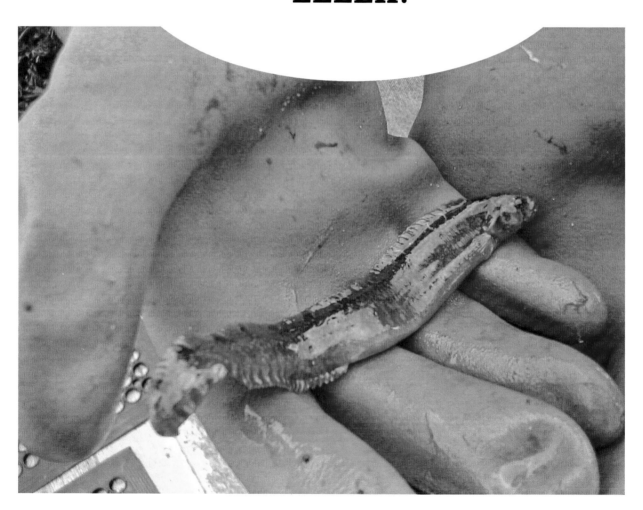

Sometimes you catch a **_scary sculpin_**. **YIKES!**

Sometimes a bright

sea star comes along

for the ride.

And
sometimes
all you catch
is a **LOT** of
seaweed!

But sometimes, when you're lucky, you catch a **LOBSTER!**

Ed plucks it from the trap.

WATCH OUT FOR ITS CLAWS, ED!

Then he replaces the empty bait bag

with a full one, and resets

the trap.

Anne's job is

to *measure* the lobster

to see if it's big enough.

It's a **KEEPER!**

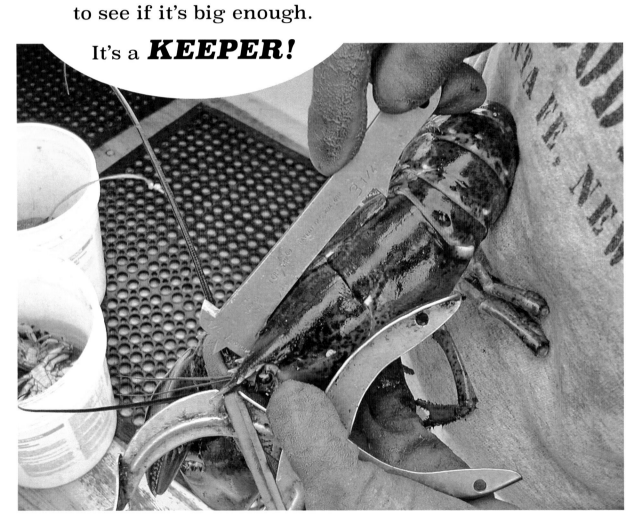

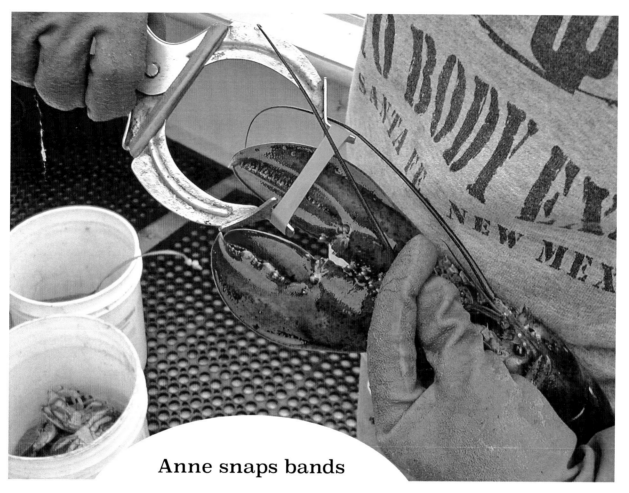

Anne snaps bands
around the lobster's claws.
This keeps it from pinching
other lobsters.
OUCH!

What a **handsome** fellow!

Here's another one.

It's a **boy**.

And another one.
It's a *girl*. Can you tell
the **difference?**

This one is a mother lobster. **WOW!** Her belly is *covered* with *eggs*.

Poor thing! She's lost a thumb.
But ***don't worry***! It will grow back
as good as new! Anne throws the big mamma back
into the water. One day her eggs will hatch
and fill the sea with little lobsters.

At the end of the day,

when Ed has checked all of his traps,

and the ***bucket is full***,

it's time to go home.

First Ed washes
the Anne Elizabeth from
bow to stern. He keeps
a *clean boat!*

Then
the family
heads home.
It's been a good
day's work
and the best is
yet to come—
lobster for
dinner
tonight!

Lobster Lore

For conservation purposes, lobsters caught in Maine must be over a minimum size (3-1/4") and under a maxmimum size (5"), measured from the rear of the eye socket to the rear end of the **carapace**, or body shell.

A mother lobster is called a **seeder** because the eggs she carries under her body are often called seeds. Depending on her age, she will carry from 6,000 to 100,000 eggs for about a year. Maine law states that when a lobsterman catches a female bearing eggs, he must **make a notch in one of her tail flippers** and return her to the water. He must also return any female whose flipper is notched, even if she is not bearing eggs. This allows her to continue to reproduce and assures the continuation of the fishery.

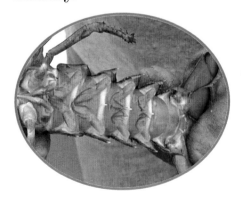

All lobsters have appendages called **swimmerets** under their tails. In a male lobster, the two closest to the legs are hard, while in a female they are soft and feathery.

Every lobsterman picks a color for his **buoy**, and he must display one on his boat so that the **marine warden** (the water police) can tell that he's pulling the right traps. Each buoy can be tied to one or more traps, up to 15, depending on where he fishes in Maine.

This is a **tag** that must be fastened to each lobster trap; it's like a car license plate since it identifies the owner of a trap. In most areas of Maine, each lobster license holder may have up to **800 traps**.

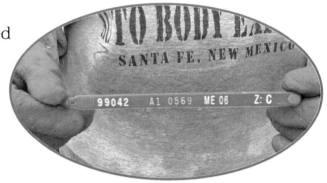

Lobsters crawl in either end of the trap and end up in the **"kitchen"** where the bait is. They become confused as to which way to go to get out of the trap and continue along into another part of the trap where they are when the trap is pulled to the surface. The bright pink **escape vent** is sized to allow juvenile and undersized lobsters out of the trap. The vent will eventually fall off if a trap is lost on the bottom of the ocean so that all lobsters can get out.

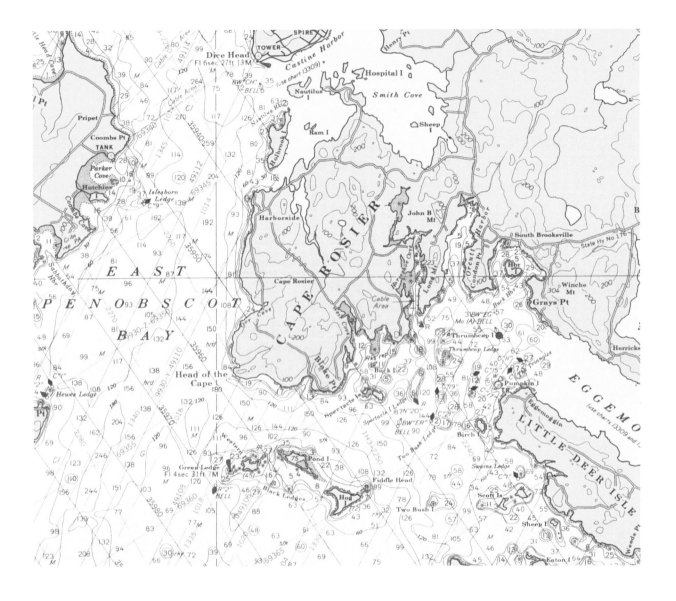

Nautical chart of the portion of Penobscot Bay, Maine, where Ed Black lobsters, from the Image Archives of the Historical Map & Chart Collection/Office of Coast Survey/National Ocean Service/NOAA.

Photographs by Leslie Moore with additional photos courtesy of Penobscot Bay Press, Inc.